The Orphan Train
An Original Musical in One Act

Book
Susan Nanus & Sasha Nanus

Lyrics
Susan Nanus

Music
Barbara Anselmi

A Samuel French Acting Edition

SAMUELFRENCH.COM
SAMUELFRENCH-LONDON.CO.UK

Book Copyright © 2005, 2013 by Susan Nanus and Sasha Nanus
Lyrics Copyright © 2005, 2013 by Susan Nanus
All Rights Reserved
Cover Image © Leigh *and* Perfect Gui/Shutterstock

THE ORPHAN TRAIN is fully protected under the copyright laws of the United States of America, the British Commonwealth, including Canada, and all other countries of the Copyright Union. All rights, including professional and amateur stage productions, recitation, lecturing, public reading, motion picture, radio broadcasting, television and the rights of translation into foreign languages are strictly reserved.

ISBN 978-0-573-70121-4

www.SamuelFrench.com
www.SamuelFrench-London.co.uk

For Production Enquiries

United States and Canada
Info@SamuelFrench.com
1-866-598-8449

United Kingdom and Europe
Theatre@SamuelFrench-London.co.uk
020-7255-4302

Each title is subject to availability from Samuel French, depending upon country of performance. Please be aware that *THE ORPHAN TRAIN* may not be licensed by Samuel French in your territory. Professional and amateur producers should contact the nearest Samuel French office or licensing partner to verify availability.

CAUTION: Professional and amateur producers are hereby warned that *THE ORPHAN TRAIN* is subject to a licensing fee. Publication of this play(s) does not imply availability for performance. Both amateurs and professionals considering a production are strongly advised to apply to Samuel French before starting rehearsals, advertising, or booking a theatre. A licensing fee must be paid whether the title(s) is presented for charity or gain and whether or not admission is charged. Professional/Stock licensing fees are quoted upon application to Samuel French.

No one shall make any changes in this title(s) for the purpose of production. No part of this book may be reproduced, stored in a retrieval system, or transmitted in any form, by any means, now known or yet to be invented, including mechanical, electronic, photocopying, recording, videotaping, or otherwise, without the prior written permission of the publisher. No one shall upload this title(s), or part of this title(s), to any social media websites.

For all enquiries regarding motion picture, television, and other media rights, please contact Samuel French.

MUSIC USE NOTE

Licensees are solely responsible for obtaining formal written permission from copyright owners to use copyrighted music in the performance of this play and are strongly cautioned to do so. If no such permission is obtained by the licensee, then the licensee must use only original music that the licensee owns and controls. Licensees are solely responsible and liable for all music clearances and shall indemnify the copyright owners of the play(s) and their licensing agent, Samuel French, against any costs, expenses, losses and liabilities arising from the use of music by licensees. Please contact the appropriate music licensing authority in your territory for the rights to any incidental music.

RENTAL MATERIALS

An orchestration consisting of **Piano/Vocal Score** will be loaned two months prior to the production ONLY on the receipt of the Licensing Fee quoted for all performances, the rental fee and a refundable deposit.

Please contact Samuel French for perusal of the music materials as well as a performance license application.

IMPORTANT BILLING AND CREDIT REQUIREMENTS

If you have obtained performance rights to this title, please refer to your licensing agreement for important billing and credit requirements.

THE ORPHAN TRAIN was originally produced at The Jewish Community Center in Manhattan in association with the Anti Defamation League, a New York Jewish Teen Theatre production. The Musical Director was Barbara Anselmi, with Choreography by David Beris, Costumes by Rebecca Rosenstreich, Art work by Allison Fox, Set Construction by Frank Uvino, Hilda Valencia, Basil Latore and David Vazquez. The Postcard designer was David Billotti and the Design Staff was Nancy Hartner and Shin Horikawa. The production was directed by Sasha Nanus with the following cast:

RACHEL	Rachel Mann
JESSIE/JESSICA	Lucy Batterman
JOHNNY	Johnny Fernandez
YUSI	Yusi Ramirez
ANNI	Wei Ying Zeng
CARLOS	David Pereira
KATHY	Eliana Lane
MARY	Jennifer Wachs
ANGELA	Annie Siegel
JACK	Ray Sultan
RAY	Ethan Stanislawski
LAURA	Maren Silberstein
MOLLY	Natasha Thompson
MATT	Jonathan Katz

CHARACTERS

Rachel

Jessie/Jessica

Harlem Gang

Johnny

Annie

Yusi

Carlos

Maria

Hell's Kitchen Gang

Jack

Mary

Ray

Kathy

Angela

Conductor

Rich Kids

Isabel

Charlotte

Louisa

Matt

Molly

Laura

MUSICAL NUMBERS

Scene 1 - Rachel's Bedroom
1 *My Life* .... Rachel & Jessica

Scene 2 - Union Station, New York City
2 *The Name of The Game* .... Orphans

Scene 2A - Train to Kansas
3 *Orphan Train* .... Orphans & Rachel
4 *No Different*........................... Rachel & Orphans

Scene 3 - A Town Square
5 *In This Town*................................ Kansas Kids
6 *In This Town (Reprise)*.......................... Orphans

Scene 4 - Various Homes
7 *Things Aren't Always What They Seem*.................... Cast

Scene 5 - Jessie's House
8 *Jessie's Song*............................. Jessie & Rachel

Scene 6 - Jessie's House, Another Day

Scene 7 - The Barn
9 *Hoe Down*... Cast
10 *New York City Beat*................................ Cast

Scene 8 - Train Station

Scene Change
11 *My Life* .... Instrumental

Scene 9 - Rachel's Bedroom
12 *Things Aren't Always What They Seem (Reprise)* .... Cast

Bows
13 *Orphan Train* .... Cast

Scene 1- Rachel's Bedroom

(Lights up on **RACHEL**, *alone in her room working on homework.)*

RACHEL. Oh forget it! I'm sick of this!

JESSICA. *(as she walks into the room)* I downloaded a bunch of movies on my iPad. I've really gotten into oldies lately. Have you ever seen *Casablanca*?

(She realizes that **RACHEL** *is in a bad mood.)*

What's the matter?

RACHEL. Nothing.

JESSICA. Yes, there is. What's going on?

RACHEL. Forget it. You wouldn't understand.

JESSICA. Did I do something? Are you mad at me?

RACHEL. Why would I be mad at you?

JESSICA. Well, who are you mad at?

RACHEL. Myself. For being born into the wrong family.

JESSICA. What?

RACHEL. I'm not like the rest of them. By the way, did you bring your math homework?

JESSICA. Yeah.

RACHEL. Hand it over. I need to copy it.

JESSICA. Rachel…

RACHEL. What?

JESSICA. You know I don't like to give out my homework. I did a lot of work on it and it doesn't seem fair that you should just copy it.

RACHEL. Oh. I see. In other words, you're as selfish as my parents. If I were as smart as you are, I'd be happy to give you my homework. Unfortunately, I'm stupid, and not that you care, but if I bring home a bad report card again, I'll be grounded for the rest of the year.

JESSICA. You're not stupid. You don't even try. I bet you could get A's and B's if you'd just work at it a little…

RACHEL. *A little?* My brother is at Harvard and my sister is at Yale. There is no "little" in this family. Either you're outstanding or you're nothing. And guess which one I am.

JESSICA. That's not true.

RACHEL. Everyone expects me to follow in their footsteps, but I'm not like them.

(SONG - "My Life")

(sings)

FROM THE MOMENT I WAKE UP
TILL I GO TO BED AT NIGHT
I FEEL ALL THIS PRESSURE
TO DO EVERYTHING RIGHT
GET PERFECT GRADES
WIN EVERY PRIZE
STAND OUT FROM THE CROWD
NO MATTER THE SIZE.

I HATE MY LIFE
IT NEVER FEELS RIGHT
I FEEL SO LONELY INSIDE

DON'T HAVE ANY GOALS
NO SPECIAL DREAM.
IF ONE MORE PERSON ASKS ME
I THINK I'M GONNA SCREAM.

DON'T KNOW WHO I AM
OR WHERE I MIGHT FIT
I FEEL LESS LIKE A PERSON
AND MORE LIKE AN "IT."

I HATE MY LIFE
IT NEVER FEELS RIGHT
I FEEL SO LONELY INSIDE.

JESSICA.
>I'M REALLY SORRY, RACHEL
>IF THAT'S HOW YOU FEEL.

RACHEL.
>NOTHING HAS MEANING
>NOTHING IS REAL.

JESSICA.
>I THINK YOU SHOULD TALK TO SOMEONE
>MAYBE A SHRINK?

RACHEL.
>I'VE BEEN TO FIFTEEN,
>AND BELIEVE ME, THEY STINK!
>I FEEL SO LONELY INSIDE

JESSICA.
>FEEL SO LONELY INSIDE

RACHEL.
>I FEEL SO USELESS INSIDE

JESSICA.
>SO USELESS INSIDE

RACHEL.
>LIKE A FAILURE INSIDE

JESSICA.
>LIKE A FAILURE INSIDE

RACHEL.
>I HATE MY LIFE. IT NEVER FEELS RIGHT.

JESSICA. Wow, I'm sorry, Rachel. I had no idea. But there's got to be a solution, right? There has to be something you can do.

RACHEL. There is.

JESSICA. You're going to talk to your parents? Tell them how you feel? Or maybe you should write a letter. Sometimes when they see it in writing, it really sinks in.

RACHEL. You're right. I should write a note before I leave.

JESSICA. Leave?

RACHEL. I'm getting out of here, Jess.

JESSICA. What are you talking about?

RACHEL. I've got some money saved up. Tomorrow morning, I'm going to get on a train and see where it takes me.

JESSICA. Are you crazy? You're only fifteen! You can't just take off.

RACHEL. Lots of kids do it.

JESSICA. Yeah, and bad things happen to them!

RACHEL. I'm suffocating here, Jess. I have to figure out who the real me is, and where I belong and what I'm supposed to be doing.

JESSICA. Rachel, think about this…

RACHEL. I have, and my mind is made up.

JESSICA. Your parents are going to be so upset.

RACHEL. Actually, I think they'll be relieved.

(She pulls down a suitcase from the top shelf. It falls and bumps her on the head.)

JESSICA. Oh my God! Are you all right?

RACHEL. Huh? What? I'm fine.

(She rubs her head but starts packing.)

JESSICA. You see? It's too dangerous!

RACHEL. I can take care of myself.

JESSICA. You don't know that. You've never really been on your own.

RACHEL. Tell you what. I'll call you in a couple of days. And let you know how I'm doing.

JESSICA. A couple of days! That's insane! You have to call me the second you get off the train!

RACHEL. Fine, I will! And if things aren't going well, you can tell my parents where I am; otherwise, you have to promise to keep quiet.

JESSICA. Rachel…

RACHEL. Please, Jess. I have to do this. I'll be all right.

JESSICA. *(reluctantly)* Okay, but swear you'll call me.

RACHEL. Swear.

(They hug and as they break apart, **RACHEL** *swoons a bit.)*

Wow, I better sit down for a second. My head really hurts.

JESSICA. Rachel! You can't go. You can barely stand.

RACHEL. I'm fine. Just give me a minute.

(She sits as lights fade.)

Scene 2 - Union Station

CONDUCTOR. *(shouts)* The Cannonball Express leaving for Chicago, St. Louis, Topeka, and Los Angeles leaves on Track 99 in fifteen minutes. All aboard!

(**JOHNNY, CARLOS, YUSI, ANNIE,** *and* **MARIA,** *all teenagers, all dressed in ragged clothes from the 1920's, enter.*)

YUSI. Why can't we live on our own. They gonna put us on a stupid farm.

MARIA. Why can't we stay by ourselves.

JOHNNY. What are you talking about? You had the influenza last winter you almost croaked.

MARIA. I wish my momma was still around.

ANNIE. What happened to her again?

MARIA. Working in that factory all her life. Her lungs gave out.

JOHNNY. All right you guys, stop your cry babying. We're looking to the future now and everything is gonna be ok.

ANNIE. Where do you think they're sending us, Johnny?

YUSI. How should he know? Is he a mind reader?

CARLOS. They gonna give us any food on this trip?

YUSI. It don't matter if they do. You'll still be hungry. You're always hungry.

CARLOS. Can I help it if I'm a growing boy?

MARIA. *(pulls out a baguette from her bag)* Look what I stole!

(Everyone starts grabbing for it and ad lib that they want a piece.)

JOHNNY. Quit grabbing! There's enough for everyone!

(They all huddle in the corner sharing the bread.)

(**IRISH KIDS** – **JACK, MARY, RAY, KATHY, ANGELA** – *enter.*)

JACK. Now remember, everybody watch out for each other. Don't go talkin' to no strangers. You never know who you can trust.

MARY. I'm scared, Jack. Why are they sending us away? I don't want to go. What if nobody wants us?

RAY. You worry too much.

KATHY. Don't you worry, Mary. They wouldn't be sending us to Kansas if they didn't have no homes for us, would they?

ANGELA. I lit a candle in church yesterday asking my folks in heaven to watch over us.

JACK. That's nice, Angela. Next time, say a prayer for me.

ANGELA. Yeah, but what if they're mean? What if they beat us?

KATHY. You both have great imaginations. It's going to be good. Anything's better than having no family at all, ain't it?

ANGELA. I guess so…

RAY. *(sees the other kids)* Oh oh.

MARY. What's the matter?

RAY. *(points)* Look.

(They all look over at the others.)

JACK. Don't tell me they're on our train!

*(**CARLOS** and the others turn and notice them.)*

JOHNNY. Well, well, look who's here. Irish Jack.

JACK. You're a long way from Harlem, Johnny.

CARLOS. You guys must be lost. This ain't Hell's Kitchen.

JOHNNY. Every neighborhood is hell when those Micks are around.

*(The **HARLEM KIDS** laugh.)*

ANNIE. Hey, Mary.

MARY. Hi, Annie.

ANGELA. Don't talk to her!

MARY. Why not? She's nice. I've seen her around on the streets.

ANGELA. Nobody from Harlem is nice.

YUSI. Well that goes double for anybody from Hell's Kitchen.

KATHY. Oh, yeah? Well, that goes triple for anybody from Harlem!

(SONG - "The Name of Game")

(sings)

I LOOK IN THE MIRROR AND WHAT DO I SEE?
A REAL IRISH FACE LOOKIN' RIGHT BACK AT ME.
I LOOK AT MY FRIENDS
AND THEY LOOK THE SAME.
DON'T MIX WITH STRANGERS IS THE NAME OF THE GAME!

YUSI.

MY FRIENDS AND MY FOLKS, WE DO WHAT WE MUST
TO KEEP AWAY FROM OUTSIDERS
WHO YOU CAN'T EVER TRUST.
STICK TO YOUR OWN KIND,
THAT'S WHAT WE CLAIM.
DON'T MIX WITH STRANGERS IS THE NAME OF THE GAME.

IRISH KIDS.

YOUR FOODS AND YOUR CUSTOMS
ARE ALL VERY ODD
WE PREFER TO BE LIKE PEAS IN A POD.

HARLEM KIDS.

YOUR MUSIC SOUNDS WEIRD
YOU DON'T KNOW HOW TO DANCE.
WHY SHOULD WE BOTHER GIVING STRANGERS A CHANCE?

CARLOS & JOHNNY.

WHEN I WALK AROUND IN MY NEIGHBORHOOD,
I SEE PEOPLE LIKE ME
AND THAT FEELS REAL GOOD.
OUR HERITAGE AND HISTORY
PUTS YOURS TO SHAME.

HARLEM KIDS.
DON'T MIX WITH STRANGERS.
IRISH KIDS.
DON'T MIX WITH STRANGERS.

(Dance Challenge:

Some of the Harlem kids dance while the rest of their group cheers them on.

Now some of the Irish Kids dance as a challenge! The rest of their group cheers them on!)

ALL.
SO YOU STICK TO YOUR KIND, I'LL STICK TO MINE,
JUST LEAVE ME ALONE
AND WE'LL ALL BE FINE.
WE'LL KEEP TO OURSELVES AND YOU DO THE SAME.
HARLEM KIDS.
DON'T MIX WITH
IRISH KIDS.
DON'T MIX WITH
ALL.
DON'T TALK OR TOLERATE
HARLEM KIDS.
DON'T MIX WITH
IRISH KIDS.
DON'T MIX WITH
ALL.
DON'T TALK OR TOLERATE
DON'T MIX WITH STRANGERS
IS THE NAME OF THE GAME!

CONDUCTOR. Last call for the Cannonball Express! All aboard! Hey! What are you kids doing on the platform? Get on the train! We're leaving in two minutes.

KATHY. We still got two minutes. Keep your shirt on. You don't have to be so pushy.

CONDUCTOR. I'll be any way I want to, you little street beggar. Get going!

(The kids start to step through the door of the train.)

RAY. Hey, This is a boxcar! Where are we supposed to sit?

CONDUCTOR. On the floor and don't give me none of your lip. You should be thankful for anything you get!

*(Kids continue to go into train as **JOHNNY** and **KATHY** bump into each other.)*

KATHY. Why don't you watch where you're going!

JOHNNY. Sorry, Kathy, I didn't mean to bump into you.

KATHY. How do you know my name?

JOHNNY. I seen you around and I asked about you. I'm Johnny.

KATHY. Really.

JOHNNY. Whenever somethin' interests me, I like to get more information.

KATHY. Oh yeah? And what information did you get?

JOHNNY. That you're fourteen, that you've been living on the streets for two years, and you take care of yourself.

KATHY. Well, aren't you a regular detective.

*(**JACK** steps out of the train with **MARY** trailing behind him.)*

JACK. Hey! What are you doing with my sister?

JOHNNY. Irish Jack is your brother?

JACK. You better believe it, and she don't want nothin' to do with you. C'mon.

KATHY. I have a right to talk to whoever I want to!

JACK. No you don't. Now let's go!

(They start to enter the boxcar.)

MARY. C'mon, sit with me.

*(At that moment, **RACHEL** enters with her suitcase.)*

RACHEL. Excuse me, I'm looking for the Cannonball Express.

CONDUCTOR. Where did you come from?

RACHEL. The ticket booth. I want to go to...

CONDUCTOR. I know where you're goin'. Get in there with the rest of them kids!

RACHEL. Actually, I paid for a sleeper car.

CONDUCTOR. Did you now? You'll sleep just fine in there.

RACHEL. It was a private sleeper car.

CONDUCTOR. Did you hear what I said, missy? Move!

*(Intimidated, **RACHEL** enters the boxcar and sees all the other kids.)*

RACHEL. Wait a minute! This is a mistake!

*(The **CONDUCTOR** closes the door and locks it.)*

What are you doing? This is not a sleeper car! Let me out of here!

(We hear the sound of a train whistle. Everyone mimes being lurched by the train and then bounces up and down very slightly as if the train is moving.)

RACHEL. *(yells)* You are in big trouble, mister! I'm going to report you to the manager! *(She turns and looks around.)* I don't believe this! Where are the seats?

CARLOS. Orphans don't get no seats.

RACHEL. Excuse me?

KATHY. When you're poor and you ain't got no parents, everybody treats you like dirt. So we gotta sit on the floor.

RACHEL. There must be some mistake. I'm not poor and I am definitely not an orphan.

YUSI. Yeah, I used to play that game, too. I'd pretend I was a princess and my mama and daddy were the king and queen.

RACHEL. I don't have to pretend anything. I'm telling the truth.

KATHY. Then why are you on the Orphan Train?

RACHEL. The what?

(SONG - "Orphan Train")

KATHY. *(sings)*
    IF YOU'RE A KID AND YOU LIVE ON THE STREET,
    YOUR PARENTS ARE DEAD,
    YOU GOT NOTHIN' TO EAT,
    YOU STEAL FOR A LIVING
    YOU DON'T GO TO SCHOOL.
    THE COPS AND THE JUDGES CAME UP WITH THIS RULE:

JACK.
    THEY PUT YOU ON THE ORPHAN TRAIN.
    AND SEND YOU OUT WEST.
    DON'T BOTHER TO COMPLAIN,
    BECAUSE THEY THINK THEY KNOW BEST.
    THEY DON'T EVEN ASK YOU
    JUST MAKE AN ARREST
    AND DRAG YOU TO THE STATION AND PUT YOU ON THE
        ORPHAN TRAIN.

RACHEL. Out West? Where?

ANGELA. Some place in Kansas.

RACHEL. *(horrified)* Kansas! I bought a ticket to Los Angeles!

RAY.
    IF YOU'RE A KID AND YOU AIN'T GOT A BUCK,
    DON'T MATTER WHAT YOU WANT,
    YOU'RE PLUMB OUT OF LUCK.
    YOU AIN'T GOT NO RIGHTS AND
    YOU DON'T HAVE NO SAY
    THE PEOPLE WITH POWER DON'T WANT YOU TO STAY.

MARY.
    SO THEY PUT YOU ON THE ORPHAN TRAIN
    AND SEND YOU OUT WEST.
    DON'T BOTHER TO COMPLAIN,
    BECAUSE THEY THINK THEY KNOW BEST.
    THEY DON'T EVEN ASK
    THE JUST MAKE AN ARREST
    AND DRAG YOU TO THE STATION AND PUT YOU ON THE
        ORPHAN TRAIN.

RACHEL.
> I DON'T UNDERSTAND. I'M REALLY PERPLEXED.
> THEY SEND YOU TO KANSAS AND WHAT HAPPENS NEXT?

YUSI.
> WE GET ADOPTED. GET A NEW MOM AND DAD.

ANNIE.
> ADOPTED. WHICH CAN BE GOOD OR BAD.

YUSI.
> ADOPTED. A FAMILY OF OUR OWN.

RACHEL.
> BUT I HAVE A FAMILY! I WANT TO BE ALONE.

JOHNNY.
> IF YOU'RE A KID, YOU HAVE LOTS OF HOPE,
> THEN YOU GET WISE.
> AND STOP BEING A DOPE.
> THEY CALL IT ADOPTION,
> BUT I CALL IT JAIL.

ANGELA.
> THERE'S NO ESCAPE,
> NO WAY TO POST BAIL.

ALL.
> THEY PUT YOU ON THE ORPHAN TRAIN
> AND SEND YOU OUT WEST.
> DON'T BOTHER TO COMPLAIN,
> BECAUSE THEY THINK THEY KNOW BEST.
> THEY DON'T EVEN ASK
> JUST MAKE AN ARREST
> AND DRAG YOU TO THE STATION AND PUT YOU ON THE ORPHAN
> AND DRAG YOU TO THE STATION AND PUT YOU ON THE ORPHAN
> AND DRAG YOU TO THE STATION AND PUT YOU ON THE ORPHAN
> TRAIN.

RACHEL. This is horrible! I have to get off this train.

CARLOS. You can't. Didn't you see the man lock the door?

RACHEL. We'll see about that. I'm going to call 911.

(She opens her knapsack and searches through it and pulls out her cell phone and tries to turn it on. It doesn't work.)

What is the matter with this thing? I just recharged it.

YUSI. Excuse me, but what is that thing?

RACHEL. My cell phone, of course. *(shakes it)* Why doesn't it work?

JACK. What's a cell phone?

RACHEL. Hello-oh. A cellular telephone? Where have you been living?

RAY. That itty bitty thing is a telephone? Where are the wires?

RACHEL. Honestly, you people. Where have you been for the last ten years?

(They take her comment literally and try to remember.)

JOHNNY. I got it! Ten years ago, we were celebrating the end of the war.

JACK. That's right. The Armistice.

RACHEL. War? What war?

KATHY. The Great War, of course.

RACHEL. You mean the war on terror?

KATHY. NO, the war to end all wars in 1918.

RACHEL. Nineteen-eighteen? What are you talking about?

JOHNNY. You really never had no schoolin', did you? It's simple arithmetic. If it's 1928 now, then ten years ago it was 1918.

RACHEL. Are you telling me that we are in the year 1928? And the war ten years ago was World War One?

KATHY. I never heard it called that.

JACK. Maybe she thinks there's going to be a World War Two.

(They all laugh at how absurd that is.)

RACHEL. Who's the President of the United States?

RAY. Calvin Coolidge, of course.

RACHEL. Who's the most popular movie star?

MARY. John Barrymore. He's so dreamy.

RACHEL. What's your favorite TV show?

CARLOS. What's TV?

ANNIE. I ain't never even seen a show!

RACHEL. What's your favorite music?

MARIA. Charleston, of course.

(She starts dancing to the Charleston and grabs one of the kids.)

RACHEL. What is going on here?

ANGELA. What'cha mean what's going on? Same as all of us! You're getting adopted.

RACHEL. Oh, my God! This is crazy. This is horrible! How did I get on this train?

JACK. The same way everyone else did. So, I guess you'll want to be sitting with us, eh, Rachel? A good Irish girl like yourself.

RACHEL. Excuse me?

YUSI. You don't know that for sure. She might have some African blood in her.

RACHEL. African blood? Not that I know of.

JACK. See? I knew it.

RACHEL. But I'm not Irish, either. I'm Jewish.

ANNIE. Jewish!

YUSI. Holy Mary mother of God! I ain't never seen a Jew before.

RACHEL. Actually, we look just like anybody else.

ANGELA. Does that mean you don't celebrate Christmas?

RACHEL. I celebrate Chanukah.

MARY. What about Easter?

RACHEL. We have Passover.

YUSI. I knew a Jewish kid once. He was okay.

MARIA. But don't you wear funny hats?

ANNIE. And don't Jews speak a different language?

RACHEL. Well, do you mean Yiddish? Or Russian? My grandparents came from Russia. Where did yours come from?

JOHNNY. My parents came from Cuba.

ANGELA. Ireland.

JACK. Wish we had the luck of the Irish, right, Kathy?

(KATHY nods.)

CARLOS. I think we're from Turkey.

ANNIE. I know where I'm from. Italy! I could go for some pasta right now.

MARY. Pasta? Forget about it. Roasted potatoes! That's the ticket.

RACHEL. Didn't your families speak different languages too?

JOHNNY. Come to think of it, my buela spoke Spanish.

RACHEL. We all came from somewhere, you know.

CARLOS. Are you rich?

RACHEL. Why would you say that?

CARLOS. All Jews are rich, ain't they?

RACHEL. Not at all. My dad's a teacher. My brother and sister go to school on scholarships. My grandfather was a rag peddler.

RAY. That don't sound rich to me.

(SONG - "No Different")

RACHEL. *(sings)*
RICH OR POOR.
DARK EYES OR LIGHT.
SOME HAVE OLIVE SKIN
SOME HAVE WHITE
PEOPLE WONDER
WHAT'S A JEW?
THEY'RE NO DIFFERENT FROM YOU OR YOU.

SOME HAVE CURLY HAIR
SOME HAVE STRAIGHT
SOME ARE THIN
SOME NEED TO LOSE WEIGHT.
PEOPLE WONDER
WHAT'S A JEW?
THEY'RE NO DIFFERENT FROM YOU OR YOU.

JACK.
YOUR FOODS ARE DIFFERENT, YOUR CUSTOMS LOOK ODD.

RACHEL.
BUT LIKE CHRISTIANS AND MUSLIMS, WE SHARE THE SAME GOD.
WE HAVE RABBIS, NOT PRIESTS.
WE PRAY IN A SHUL.
BUT LIKE YOU WE FOLLOW
THE GOLDEN RULE.
THERE'S NO REASON
FOR YOU TO ATTACK,
IN FACT IN ETHIOPIA,
SOME OF US ARE BLACK!

PEOPLE WONDER
WHAT'S A JEW?
THEY'RE NO DIFFERENT
FROM ANY OF YOU.

RACHEL.
RICH OR POOR.

ORPHANS.
RICH OR POOR.

RACHEL.
DARK EYES OR LIGHT.

ORPHANS.
DARK EYES OR LIGHT.

RACHEL.
SOME HAVE OLIVE SKIN

ORPHANS.
SOME HAVE OLIVE SKIN

ALL.
>SOME HAVE WHITE
>PEOPLE WONDER

RACHEL.
>WHAT'S A JEW?
>THEY'RE NO DIFFERENT
>>FROM YOU OR YOU.
>
>SOME HAVE CURLY HAIR
>SOME HAVE STRAIGHT
>SOME ARE THIN
>SOME NEED TO LOSE
>>WEIGHT.

ORPHANS.
>OOOO OOOO

ALL.
>PEOPLE WONDER
>WHAT IS A JEW?

RACHEL.
>THEY'RE NO DIFFERENT FROM YOU OR YOU.

ALL.
>FORGET WHAT'S DIFFERENT
>LOOK HOW WE'RE THE SAME.
>TO PUT A WALL BETWEEN US
>WOULD BE A REAL SHAME.

RACHEL.
>SO IF YOU'RE WONDERING
>WHAT IS A JEW?

RACHEL.
>JUST GIVE ME A CHANCE

ORPHANS.
>JUST GIVE HER THE CHANCE

RACHEL.
>JUST GIVE ME A CHANCE

ORPHANS.
>JUST GIVE HER THE CHANCE

RACHEL.
>TO MAKE FRIENDS WITH YOU.
>
>Listen, until I figure out how I got here and how I'm getting to L.A., can't we all sit together?

JACK. Are you crazy?

JOHNNY. We don't ever sit with them.

RACHEL. Why not? In my school, I have friends of all races and we always sit together.

RAY. Well, we don't!

CARLOS. That's right. We never have and we never will!

(The KIDS start calling to RACHEL to sit with them. She raises her voice over the noise.)

RACHEL. I've made a decision and I guess I'll just have to sit in the middle.

MARY. Well, I'm going to sit next to her.

(She moves over to sit on RACHEL's right)

YUSI. So am I.

(She sits on RACHEL's left. After a moment, all the Irish Kids sit in a line next to MARY and the Harlem Kids sit in a line next to YUSI.)

RACHEL. Looks like we're kind of sitting together after all.

(Traveling music plays as the KIDS start to settle down for the night. They all curl up on their bags and suitcases except for JOHNNY and KATHY. The two of them look at each other. JOHNNY tips his cap to acknowledge KATHY. She tips her cap in response and then slowly curls up. JOHNNY sleeps sitting up. The music slows down. Lights change. JOHNNY jumps up and peers out a window.)

Scene 3 – A town square

(Before the Train arrives. The **RICH KIDS** *are waiting by the train platform.* **LOUISA** *is sketching* **ISABEL**.*)*

ISABEL. *(brushing off her clothes)* How do I look? Do I look all right?

CHARLOTTE. Oh, you look beautiful.

LOUISA. I wouldn't go that far. Stop moving!

ISABEL. I have to look good, you know. My father is the chief of police!

CHARLOTTE. I love your dress! It's so elegant.

ISABEL. This is a store-bought dress, you know. None of that boring handmade stuff. Handmade clothes are for peasants.

LOUISA. In Paris, everyone wears handmade clothes.

ISABEL. Oh, you and Paris. That's all you ever talk about.

CHARLOTTE. I'd love to go to Paris.

LOUISA. When I'm a famous artist, I'll send you a ticket.

CHARLOTTE. Thank you, Louisa! But Mama would never allow it.

*(***MOLLY** *and* **MATT** *come running in.)*

MATT. Are they here yet?

MOLLY. Obviously not, Matt. Use your eyes. You see anyone here?

ISABEL. The train is late as usual. I'll have to talk to my father about that.

*(***JESSIE** *and* **LAURA**, *a girl on cruches, walk in.)*

JESSIE. Don't you mean our father? He's the mayor and your father's boss.

ISABEL. A boss who sits behind a desk all day! My father does all the work!

LOUISA. Here we go again.

MATT. Can't you girls ever get along?

LAURA. Please don't fight today. We want to make a good impression.

MOLLY. On a bunch of orphans? Who cares what they think, anyway.

LAURA. They're going to be our new brothers and sisters.

JESSIE. We'll see about that.

LOUISA. Finished! Tada! *(She holds up the sketch. It is a very abstract picture.)*

(They all look at it.)

MATT. I think it's upside down.

MOLLY. What is that?

LOUISA. This is modern art. Haven't you ever heard of Picasso?

JESSIE. I think it looks just like you.

ISABEL. Be quiet.

JESSIE. You be quiet.

ISABEL. Don't tell me to be quiet.

LAURA. Isn't that the train?

CHARLOTTE. Where?

LAURA. Down the track?

CHARLOTTE. Shouldn't we go down to the platform and meet them?

MATT. Absolutively, Posolutely, let's go.

(They all exit.)

*(Crossfade– **ORPHANS** are getting off the train.)*

CONDUCTOR. Last stop for the Orphan Train. Everybody out! Come on, you kids, move it along!

(He watches them come out and then leaves.)

(The kids interact with each other and look around as to where they are. Each character has some business.)

LAURA. There they are!

MOLLY. Look at their clothes! Aren't they awful?

MATT. What do you expect? They're dirt poor!

LAURA. I think they look kind of nice.

JESSIE. Humph! Our servants look a lot better than those hoodlums.

ISABEL. They're gong to live with us?

LOUISA. Definitely colorful characters!

JACK. We heard that you know. We ain't deaf.

JESSIE. Ain't? What kind of grammar is that? Didn't you ever go to school?

JOHNNY. Yeah, the school of hard knocks.

JACK. Which you would definitely flunk.

ISABEL. What's that smell?

MOLLY. It's them.

ANGELA. You try traveling in a box car for five days and see how you smell!

MOLLY. Yeah, you stuck up snobs.

ISABEL. How dare you talk to me that way. Who do you think you are?

MARIA. Who do you think you are?

(SONG - "In This Town")

JESSIE. *(sings)*
WE ARE THE RICH KIDS IN THIS TOWN.
WE ARE THE COOL ONES,
THE BEST.
OUR FATHERS ARE PROFESSIONALS,
OUR MOTHERS HAVE CLASS.
AND OUR SISTERS AND BROTHERS ARE VERY WELL DRESSED.

MOLLY & MATT.
WE HAVE PERFECT MANNERS,
WE KNOW HOW TO DANCE.
IF WE DON'T LIKE YOU, YOU DON'T HAVE A CHANCE.

LAURA.
WE'LL GO TO COLLEGE,
WE'LL TRAVEL ABROAD.
EVERYTHING ABOUT US IS SOMETHING TO APPLAUD.

RICH KIDS.
>WE ARE THE RICH KIDS IN THIS TOWN,
>WE ARE THE COOL ONES,
>THE BEST.
>WE HAVE LOTS OF SERVANTS
>AND A VERY BIG HOUSE,
>ONE LOOK AT US AND YOU'LL BE IMPRESSED.

JESSIE.
>WE'RE SPOILED ROTTEN,
>WE HAVE LOTS OF TOYS
>WE ARE "SIMPLY DARLING" LITTLE GIRLS AND BOYS.
>WE GET WHAT WE WANT,
>OR WE THROW A BIG FIT,
>WE'RE VERY MEAN AND NOT SORRY ONE BIT.

RICH KIDS.
>WE ARE THE RICH KIDS IN THIS TOWN.
>WE ARE THE COOL ONES,
>WE'RE BRUTES.
>IF YOU KNOW WHAT'S GOOD FOR YOU
>YOU'LL GET RIGHT DOWN
>ON YOUR HANDS AND KNEES AND LICK OFF OUR BOOTS!
>
>IF YOU'RE SMART YOU'LL DO WHAT WE SAY
>OR YOU WON'T LIVE TO SEE ANOTHER DAY.
>
>WE'RE ACCUSTOMED TO GETTING OUR WAY
>WE ARE THE RICH KIDS IN THIS TOWN.
>ORPHANS, WATCH OUT!

RACHEL. What a bunch of brats!

ANGELA. Shh! Rachel, they'll hear you.

RACHEL. Who do they think they are? They're no better than we are.

KATHY. Yes they are.

MARY. Come on, let's face it. They're rich and we're homeless.

RACHEL. You shouldn't put yourself down. You're as good as anyone else!

CONDUCTOR. All right, you orphans. Line up for inspection!

*(All the kids get in line except for **RACHEL** who is still busy looking for things in her bags.)*

RACHEL. Inspection? What is this, the army?

JACK. Worse. We line up and then the rich folks look us over and decide who they want to adopt.

RACHEL. That's disgusting!

CONDUCTOR. Hey, you! Get in line or you'll be sorry!

*(**RACHEL** gets in line at the far end, but she's not happy about it and turns her back on the proceedings.)*

Okay. Now as soon as the grown-ups get here, we can begin.

JESSIE. Excuse me, sir, but there's no need to wait for our parents. We are going to inspect the orphans ourselves.

CONDUCTOR. What?

MOLLY. That's right. Jessie has a letter from her father, the mayor. Show him, Jessie.

*(**JESSIE** hands a letter to the **CONDUCTOR** who reads it.)*

CONDUCTOR. This is most irregular! But this letter is signed by the mayor and it says here that you kids have permission to inspect these orphans and take home the ones you like best. I have to make sure this is correct. You come with me. *(points to **RACHEL**)* Everyone else wait here!

*(He leaves grabbing **RACHEL** by the arm.)*

JESSIE. Well, they sure don't make orphans very attractive, do they?

LAURA. Jessie, do you have to talk that way?

JESSIE. Laura, why don't you go home. Leave this to me.

*(**LAURA** looks at her sadly and then leaves. **JESSIE** walks over to **MOLLY**.)*

Molly, I don't know if any of these orphans are good enough to pick. Maybe we could wait for another batch.

MOLLY. Really. Do we actually have to have them living in our house?

ISABEL. Jessie, this is one time I agree with you.

YUSI. You got a problem with the way we look?

JESSIE. Excuse me, I wasn't talking to you.

KATHY. I think you were. And if you got a problem with her, then you got a problem with me.

ANNIE. And with me!

MATT. *(points to* **JOHNNY***)* I want him! He looks big and strong so he can do all my chores.

JOHNNY. That's what you think! I don't do nobody's chores.

MATT. You'll do mine or you'll go hungry.

JOHNNY. I'd rather starve than work for you. We're not your servants. We're supposed to be part of your families.

MATT. Oh, come on. You actually believed that?

JOHNNY. I'll tell you what I do believe. If any one of you little snots mistreat any of us, we're all getting on the train and going straight back to New York.

MATT. Oh, really? And who's going to pay for your tickets?

JOHNNY. Well, it wouldn't be you, would it? You'd have to get Daddy's money.

MATT. Well, at least I have a "Daddy."

MARY. Hey, watch your mouth!

KATHY. Don't talk to Johnny that way!

JACK. You're gonna to pay for that remark. And it won't be with money, either.

MATT. I wasn't talking to you, mind your own business!

JACK. His business is my business.

RAY. Yeah, we stick together. You insult one of us, you insult all of us, right, guys?

JOHNNY, JACK, CARLOS. Right!

(The **ORPHANS** *line up together and face the* **RICH KIDS**.*)*

(SONG - "In This Town [Reprise]")

JOHNNY, JACK, CARLOS, RAY.
> WE ARE THE NEW KIDS IN THIS TOWN.
> MIGHT BE POOR
> DON'T TAKE GUFF.
>
> WE'VE LIVED ON THE STREET AND
> WE'VE ALL BEEN AROUND
> DON'T MESS WITH US 'CAUSE WE'RE REALLY TOUGH!

JOHNNY, JACK, CARLOS, RAY. *(cont.)*

> WE EAT WITH OUR FINGERS
> GOT HOLES IN OUR SHOES.
> DON'T EVER FIGHT US, CAUSE YOU'RE GONNA LOSE!

KATHY, YUSI, ANGELA, MARY, ANNIE.
> WE AIN'T GOT NO FAMILY,
> BUT WE'RE NEVER ALONE,
> WE'RE LOYAL TO EACH OTHER, WE TAKE CARE OF OUR OWN.
>
> WE ARE THE NEW KIDS IN THIS TOWN,
> MIGHT BE POOR
> DON'T TAKE GUFF.

KATHY.
> WE CAN BE NICE
> IF YOU LOOK DEEP DOWN,
> BUT MOSTLY WE HIDE IT 'CAUSE LIFE IS SO ROUGH.

ALL.
> IN THE WINTER WE'RE FREEZING,
> IN THE SUMMER WE'RE HOT.
> OUR IDEA OF LUXURY WOULD BE TO SLEEP ON A COT.

YUSI & MARY.
> NEVER HAD A BIRTHDAY PARTY,
> NEVER GOT ANY TOYS.
> NEVER HAD A NORMAL LIFE LIKE OTHER GIRLS AND BOYS.

ORPHANS.
> WE ARE THE NEW KIDS IN THIS TOWN,
> MIGHT BE POOR
> DON'T TAKE GUFF

GOT NO MONEY, GOT NO SCHOOLING,
GOT NO PLACE TO LAY DOWN,
BUT WE'VE GOT EACH OTHER, THAT'S MORE THAN ENOUGH!

STUCK UP MANNERS, WHO CARES ABOUT THAT.
WE'D RATHER BE POOR THAN A SNOTTY RICH BRAT.
WE KNOW WHAT'S IMPORTANT, WE KNOW WHERE IT'S AT.
WE ARE THE NEW KIDS IN THIS TOWN.

JESSIE. Are you finished? We don't want to be here all day. Since we can't leave you standing here, I guess we have to decide which home you'll be going. Hey Matt, you want first dibs?

(As **RICH KIDS** *start to walk around the* **ORPHANS**, *looking them over, lights start to fade.)*

ANGELA. *(quietly)* Don't leave me, Kathy.

KATHY. Don't worry, Angela. I'm not going to let them separate us!

(lights fade)

Scene 4 –Several homes of the Town Kids

(Lights up on **RACHEL** *and* **ANNIE**, *in* **JESSIE**'s *house.)*

RACHEL. Look, this is a big mistake. I am not an orphan.

ANNIE. You're not?

RACHEL. No. In fact, I'm not even from this time.

ANNIE. I don't understand. How did you get on the Orphan Train?

RACHEL. That is something I am still trying to figure out.

JESSIE. *(enters the room and drops her coat on the floor)* Hang up my coat. And then you can start sweeping the floor.

RACHEL. *(finally sees* **JESSIE** *for the first time)* Oh my God! Jessica! It's me, Rachel! Am I glad to see you! We've been transported into the past! Do you know how we got here?

JESSIE. What are you talking about? I've never seen you before in my life! You just got off the train. Were you sleeping the whole time?

RACHEL. Sorry, but this is so confusing. You look exactly like my best friend, Jessica.

JESSIE. I'm sure I don't! Why are you staring at me like that? That is so rude!

RACHEL. Why are you so mean to everybody? Don't you like yourself?

JESSICA. How dare you! Of course I do! As a matter of fact, I love myself!

LAURA. *(calls from offstage)* Jessie, is that you? Did you bring home one of the orphans?

*(***LAURA** *comes onstage. She walks with crutches.)*

ANNIE. Actually, she brought two.

LAURA. Hello, my name is Laura. Welcome to our home.

ANNIE. Thank you. It's nice to be here *(looks at* **JESSIE**)…I think.

RACHEL. Well finally! Someone nice! Thank you.

LAURA. I've always wanted to be part of a big family. I cannot believe I am getting two new sisters. It is wonderful. We will have so much fun. I wish I could show you the town. There are some lovely things to see.

RACHEL. Why can't you?

LAURA. Well…I need to stay home to help my mother…I don't go out that often.

RACHEL. Why not? …Is it because of your legs? What happened?

(LAURA lowers her head sadly.)

JESSIE. You fool! Be quiet! We never mention her legs!

ANNIE. Why not?

JESSIE. Why do you think? Because she can't walk! It's the worst thing that's ever happened to our family, and now Rachel has embarrassed her. Do you always have such a big mouth?

RACHEL. *(apologetically)* Unfortunately, I do.

(Lights fade. Lights up on MATT, JACK, and JOHNNY, entering MATT's house. JACK and JOHNNY look around.)

JACK. Wow! This house is huge!

JOHNNY. Look at all the fancy pictures on the wall. And the piano. I always wanted to learn to play the piano.

JACK. Get a load of those stained glass windows. I feel like I'm in a church. What's in here? Another room?

MATT. Don't touch that door!

(JACK opens the door and it falls off.)

JOHNNY. Nice going, Jack.

JACK. Don't blame me! The hinges are broken.

(He sits on a chair and it breaks. JOHNNY laughs. MATT looks upset.)

This place is falling apart!

MATT. It is not!

JOHNNY. *(looks around)* You're right. Everything in this big fancy house is broken.

MATT. I tried to fix it! But I'm not good with my hands.

JACK. What about your dad?

MATT. My father left us six months ago. Mother's too proud to tell anyone, so we just pretend that he's away on business. Things around here keep getting worse and worse, but she refuses to ask anyone for help.

JOHNNY. You got any tools?

MATT. There's a whole pile in the woodshed, but I don't know what half of them are used for.

JOHNNY. You any good at fixin' things, Jack?

JACK. Is a duck good at quacking? Lead us to your hammer and nails, sonny boy, and these two orphans will show you a thing or two.

MATT. You mean you two will help me?

JOHNNY. If you stop acting like a snot-nose little jerk.

MATT. I will! I promise.

*(Lights fade on the boys. Lights up on **MOLLY**, **YUSI**, and **MARY** in **MOLLY**'s house.)*

MOLLY. Come on in. This is my bedroom.

YUSI. Your mother seemed real nice. Your father, too.

MARY. Yeah, how did you turn out to be so mean and nasty?

MOLLY. That's not a very nice thing to say!

MARY. I believe in speaking the truth. When you picked me, I was really upset. It was only after you picked Yusi, too, that I felt a little better. At least, I'll have one nice sister.

YUSI. Thanks, Mary. I feel the same about you.

MOLLY. Wait a minute. I'm not really a mean person.

YUSI. You sure could've fooled us.

MOLLY. I just act that way in front of Jessie. So she'll like me and be my friend.

MARY. You shouldn't have to act at all. A real friend likes you for who you are.

YUSI. A real friend accepts you and doesn't try to make you change.

MOLLY. Gee, that sounds nice. How long have you two been friends?

*(**MARY** and **YUSI** look at each other and laugh.)*

MARY. A couple of days.

MOLLY. That's all? You could have fooled me.

YUSI. Just like you fooled us. You're actually pretty nice. I guess things are not always what they seem.

(SONG - "Things Aren't Always What They Seem")

(sings)

SEE A TREE IN WINTER,
ITS BRANCHES ARE BARE.
IT'S EASY TO SUSPECT
THAT NOTHING'S GROWING THERE.

MARY.

BUT WAIT UNTIL SPRING
AND LIKE OUT OF A DREAM.
THERE'S A TREE FULL OF BLOSSOMS.
THINGS AREN'T ALWAYS WHAT THEY SEEM.

MOLLY.

YOU WANT TO MAKE NEW FRIENDS
BUT YOU'RE FEELING TOO SHY
YOU ACT COLD AND ALOOF
BUT INSIDE YOU WANT TO CRY.

YUSI.

JUST HOLD OUT YOUR HAND
BELIEVE IN YOUR DREAM.

MOLLY, YUSI, MARY.

AND PEOPLE WILL LIKE YOU
THINGS AREN'T ALWAYS WHAT THEY SEEM.

*(Lights up on **MATT**, **JOHNNY**, and **JACK** are working with hammers.)*

MATT, JOHNNY, JACK.
IF YOU NEED HELP,
IT'S OKAY TO ASK,
WHEN YOU WORK TOGETHER
IT'S NOT SUCH A HARD TASK.

IF YOU'RE TIRED OR AFRAID
OR IF YOU RUN OUT OF STEAM
DON'T BE ASHAMED
THINGS AREN'T ALWAYS WHAT THEY SEEM.

(**ISABEL** *and* **ANGELA** *walk in.*)

ISABEL. Well, here we are.

ANGELA. *(looking around)* This is your house? How many people live here?

ISABEL. Just three. Mother, Father, and me.

ANGELA. Three people in this palace?

ISABEL. Actually, most of the time, it's just me. Father is always at the office and Mother has her society meetings. But that's fine. I like being alone.

ANGELA. You do? I hate being alone. What do you do all day?

ISABEL. Well, there's school and my piano lessons and ballet and I read a lot.

ANGELA. I love to read. I used to go the library sometimes and stay all day. I was in the middle of *Jane Eyre* when they picked me up and put me on the Orphan Train.

ISABEL. *Jane Eyre*'s one of my favorites! *(dreamily)* Oh, that Mr. Rochester.

ANGELA. I know! He was so dashing. What happened at the end? Did he and Jane ever see each other again?

ISABEL. Wouldn't you like to find out for yourself? We have it here in our library.

ANGELA. You have your own library?

ISABEL. Over five hundred books and you can read as many as you want.

ANGELA. Pinch me. I think I just died and went to Heaven!

(LOUISA, CHARLOTTE, and MARIA are at a picnic with a basket of food.)

(MARIA is stuffing herself.)

MARIA. This is delicious! You got any more?

CHARLOTTE. You sure are hungry.

MARIA. Ya never know when you're gonna get another meal. *(puts a piece of bread in her pocket)*

LOUISA. In Paris, all the great artists starved.

MARIA. Then I'm glad I'm from New York City.

CHARLOTTE. You're from New York?

MARIA. Born and raised!

LOUISA. What's it like? Have you ever been to the Statue of Liberty?

MARIA. Sure! I seen it a couple of times.

CHARLOTTE. What about Broadway?

MARIA. I never saw a show but I've been on Fifth Avenue. The Easter parade! You should've seen them hats!

LOUISA. Tell us! Tell us! All about the fashions.

CHARLOTTE. Have you ever seen anyone famous?

MARIA. Can I have some more chicken first?

(They hand her the basket eagerly.)

ALL FIVE GIRLS.
JUST TAKE A STEP, YOU MIGHT BE SURPRISED
THINGS WE HAVE IN COMMON, DON'T NEED TO BE DISGUISED

ANGELA & ISABEL.
IF YOU WANT TO TURN A PAGE,

CHARLOTTE, LOUISA, & MARIA.
CREATE A NEW COLOR SCHEME,

ALL.
DON'T BE AFRAID,
THINGS AREN'T ALWAYS WHAT THEY SEEM.

(KATHY and MARY stand in front of their house.)

MARY. Is this for real? We really have families now?

KATHY. It's gonna be official, Mary. We got lucky. A new mom and dad. It's hard to believe.

MARY. I'm so happy I'm with you, Kathy. I was afraid I'd be alone or they'd put me with one of the kids from Harlem. But I was so wrong about Yusi.

KATHY. Don't be so afraid of everything. I told you it'd work out. And you know what? I never thought I would say this, but those kids from Harlem aren't so bad. That Johnny sure put those kids in their place!

(CARLOS and RAY enter.)

CARLOS. Kathy! Mary! Over here! Do you believe this place? It's so small. There's only one main street. Did you see those horses pulling wagons? I hate it here.

KATHY. Carlos, I know it's not New York, but what about your family? Ours are really nice.

MARY. Yeah, they really seem happy to have us. And guess what! We got our own bedroom. And all the food we can eat!

KATHY. Isn't it nice having a roof over your head and a bed to sleep in?

CARLOS. I guess. But I don't know…I'm kind of alone there. They don't have any other kids. I don't think they know anything about kids anyway. I'm still hungry all the time.

MARY. Why don't you just ask for more food?

CARLOS. I couldn't do that!

KATHY. But you should! They're your new family now. They wouldn't want you to starve.

RAY. That's what I've been telling him, but he's so stubborn. My family is great. I have chores to do, but I got my own horse! A horse! I never had a pet before, not even a cat.

CARLOS. And we're gonna start school. I always wanted to learn to read and write. I guess that's a good thing.

MARY. It is a good thing. Carlos, you'll see. It'll get better. You just got to give it some time.

CARLOS. Yeah, I guess.

RAY. The best thing is that we'll all be seeing each other. A lot!

MARY, RAY, CARLOS, KATHY.
WE DIDN'T WANT TO COME
WE THOUGHT IT WOULD BE BAD.
WHO WOULD HAVE IMAGINED,.
WE'RE ALL REALLY GLAD.

PEOPLE ARE FRIENDLY,
WE'RE ALL PART OF A TEAM
THEY TREAT US LIKE FAMILY
THINGS AREN'T ALWAYS WHAT THEY SEEM.

(Lights up on **RACHEL**. **ANNIE**, **JESSIE**. **LAURA** *sits to one side)*

LAURA. I'll be with you in a minute. I just want to finish writing in my journal. I have been writing about my two new sisters.

RACHEL. But why can't she walk?

JESSIE. Well, if you must know, she was very sick for a long time. She got better but she was never able to walk again.

RACHEL. Maybe she needs physical therapy.

ANNIE. What's that?

RACHEL.
SHE SAYS SHE CAN'T WALK
IT MIGHT NOT BE TRUE
SHE MAY JUST NEED PRACTICE
HELP FROM ME AND YOU.

LAURA, DO YOU WANT TO WALK?

LAURA.
THAT IS MY DREAM!

JESSIE.
DON'T GIVE HER FALSE HOPE!

RACHEL.
THINGS AREN'T ALWAYS WHAT THEY SEEM.

ALL.
>DON'T MAKE ASSUMPTIONS
>WHO PEOPLE MIGHT BE
>LOOK DEEP INTO THEIR HEARTS
>AND THEN YOU WILL SEE.
>
>IF YOU ACCEPT US
>THEN YOU HELP US REDEEM
>THE BEST THAT'S INSIDE US
>THINGS AREN'T ALWAYS WHAT THEY SEEM!
>
>*(lights fade)*

Scene 4A – Jessie's House

(Lights up. **ANNIE** *and* **RACHEL** *are working with* **LAURA**, *trying to help her to walk without crutches.* **LAURA** *keeps struggling while leaning on the two girls.)*

RACHEL. Come on Laura, try to use your legs..

ANNIE. Once, I broke my leg and I used a cane. Maybe we could try with a cane.

LAURA. Please don't let go! I'm afraid I'll fall. Hold on to me!

*(***JESSIE*** enters and observes them and marches over to them.)*

JESSIE. What are you doing?!

RACHEL. You can see what we're doing.

ANNIE. Yeah, she just needs practice.

JESSIE. You stay away from my sister. If she wants help, she'll get it from me! Come on Laura, let me help you to your chair.

(She grabs **LAURA***'s crutches and starts to help her to her room. Lights fade.)*

Scene 5 – Jessie's House

(Lights up on **RACHEL**, **ANNIE**, *and* **LAURA** *greeting* **KATHY, MARY, ANGELA, YUSI, MARIA, CHARLOTTE, MOLLY,** *and* **LOUISA**. *When* **RACHEL** *introduces everyone, she includes all the girls.)*

RACHEL. Hello, welcome to our tea party. Laura, this is Kathy, Mary, Angela, Maria, Yusi, and I'm guessing you already know Charlotte, Louisa, and Molly.

ANNIE. This is my first tea party, I'm so excited.

MARY. Mine, too! I'm so happy to see you again, Annie.

ANNIE. Thanks. Me, too.

ANGELA. *(looking around)* Wow, what a beautiful house.

LAURA. I'm glad you like it.

RACHEL. Girls, this is Laura, Jessie's older sister. Laura, this is Kathy, Mary, Angela, and Yusi. I'm guessing you already know Molly.

LAURA. Hi, everybody, I'm so glad you could come. Has everyone met my sister, Jessie?

JESSIE. *(coldly)* We've met, all right. And I do not greet you. I do not welcome you. And I do not say hello!

KATHY. Why don't you say goodbye and get lost?

JESSIE. Because this is my house and if anyone's going to leave, it's going to be you!

KATHY. Well, if that's how you feel. I never took crap from nobody! And I'm not gonna start taking it from you! Come on guys, let's go!

LAURA. Wait! Jessie, don't be rude. These are our guests.

JESSIE. Speak for yourself. I didn't invite them. *(to* **MOLLY***)* And that goes for you, too, you traitor!

MOLLY. I am not a traitor. Why can't I be friends with everybody?

YUSI. Yeah, why don't you at least give us a chance?

JESSIE. Why? So you can take over the rest of my life? *(glares at* **RACHEL***)* It's bad enough that she's here!

RACHEL. You really need an attitude adjustment. What is your problem?

JESSIE. My problem is you! You think you can waltz in here, act like Miss Popularity and take over my friends?

RACHEL. Popular? Me?

JESSIE. Maybe you were the leader in your town, but this is my town and I am in charge here.

RACHEL. Leader! Back home, no one even knew I was alive.

JESSIE. Very funny! It's obvious that everyone listens to you. Even my own sister!

RACHEL. I just want to help her.

JESSIE. You want to help everyone! They all think you're so wonderful and they all hate me!

(She bursts into tears. All the girls are surprised and concerned and crowd around her.)

LAURA. Jessie! What's wrong?

MARY. Are you hurt?

KATHY. Maybe she's sick. You got a doctor around here?

ANNIE. You want some tea?

ANGELA. Good idea. Somebody get her a cup of tea.

MOLLY. Maybe you ought to lie down, Jessie. Do you need to rest?

JESSIE. Leave me alone!

(She moves away from them, feeling sad and alone.)

RACHEL. Come on, Let's give her some space. Why don't we start the tea party and maybe Jessie will join us later.

*(**RACHEL** escorts the girls out of the room, but she remains hidden in the doorway, watching **JESSIE**.)*

(SONG - "Jessie's Song")

JESSIE.
WHEN DID I CHANGE?
I USED TO BE NICE.
NOW I ACT NASTY AND COLD AS ICE.

JESSIE. *(cont.)*

WHY DO I DO IT?
I DON'T REALLY KNOW.
THERE'S A DEVIL INSIDE ME THAT JUST WON'T LET GO.

I FEEL SO LONELY INSIDE.

I START LOTS OF FIGHTS
I CALL PEOPLE NAMES.
I START PRIVATE CLUBS
I KICK KIDS OUT OF GAMES.

I NEVER FEEL HAPPY,
I'M USUALLY SAD,
AND IF SOMEBODY FEELS GOOD,
I GET REALLY MAD.

I FEEL SO EMPTY INSIDE.

WHERE IS THE JESSIE THAT I USED TO BE?
WHAT HAPPENED TO THE DAYS WHEN I LIKED BEING ME?
WHERE IS THE GIRL WHO WAS EVERYONE'S FRIEND?
WHERE IS THAT JESSIE? WILL I SEE HER AGAIN?

RACHEL.

FEEL LIKE CRYING INSIDE.

JESSIE.

I DON'T UNDERSTAND
THIS BEHAVIOR OF MINE.
I KNOW THAT IT'S WRONG
AND THAT I'M OUT OF LINE.

I CAN'T SEEM TO STOP
THOUGH I KNOW THAT I SHOULD.
CAN IT BE POSSIBLE
I'M JUST NO GOOD?

I FEEL SO LONELY INSIDE.

RACHEL.

FEEL SO EMPTY INSIDE.

JESSIE.

I FEEL LIKE CRYING INSIDE.

BOTH.
>FEEL SO LONELY INSIDE.

(RACHEL comes out from behind the door.)

RACHEL. You know, I'm not who you think I am. At least I wasn't. Back home I was angry, insecure, and selfish. I thought I was worthless.

JESSIE. I don't believe you.

RACHEL. It's true. You see I was really jealous of my sister and brother because I thought they were so much better than me. I hated myself and took it out on everyone else.

JESSIE. Laura is better than me. She can't even walk, but she never complains. She's sweet and kind and everyone makes such a big fuss over her, especially my parents.

RACHEL. And you feel invisible so you act like a brat to get attention. But you know what? I've learned that there are a lot better ways to get people to notice you.

JESSIE. How?

RACHEL. By helping other people. And you could start with your sister, Laura.

JESSIE. Laura?

RACHEL. Yes. You could help her learn to walk again. We could do it together.

JESSIE. *(astonished)* Do you really think that's possible?

RACHEL. I think it's worth a try, don't you?

JESSIE. *(thinks for a moment)* Absolutely.

RACHEL. Good. Now that that's settled, shall we join the other girls for tea?

(The two girls look at each other. **JESSIE** *nods.* **RACHEL** *puts her arms around* **JESSIE** *and gives her a hug and they walk off together. Lights fade.)*

SCENE 6 – Jessie's House, Another Day

(A sequence in which **RACHEL**, **JESSIE**, *and* **ANNIE** *try to help* **LAURA** *walk without her crutches.* **LAURA** *is very fearful, though she bravely tries to walk. Each time she tries, she falls. Underscored with* ***A TREE GROWS IN WINTER.****)*

*(***LAURA** *falls yet again.)*

LAURA. It's no use. I can't do it. I can't!

(She grabs her crutches and hobbles off stage. Everyone looks sad and sympathetic. L:ights fade.)

Scene 7 – A Barn

(Lights up as **MATT** *brings in two jackets and hands one to* **JACK** *and one to* **JOHNNY**.*)*

MATT. Here you go. This one's for you, Johnny, and this one's for Jack. I hope they fit. I only wore them once or twice.

JOHNNY. Thanks! We'll take care of 'em. Don't worry.

JACK. Yeah, we'll be real careful. You won't even know they were worn.

MATT. You don't have to give them back. They're yours.

JOHNNY. Are you serious?

JACK. Really?

MATT. I have a lot of jackets. It's fine.

JOHNNY. But these are too nice.

JACK. Yeah, we can't take these.

MATT. Sure you can. You're my brothers, aren't you?

*(***JACK** *and* **JOHNNY** *don't know what to say.)*

We'll leave for the dance in fifteen minutes. I have to get ready too, you know.
(He leaves.)

(The two boys try on their jackets.)

JOHNNY. How do I look?

JACK. Not bad. What about me?

JOHNNY. Well, I wouldn't run away screaming.

(They laugh.)

JACK. I guess this means we're brothers, too.

JOHNNY. I guess.

JACK. Strange. A week ago, I hated you.

JOHNNY. Not as much as I hated you…you okay with me and Kathy?

JACK. What about you and Kathy?

JOHNNY. Uh, well…I kind of sort of like her.

JACK. You do? Really? Huh. *(thinks about it)* Yeah, I'm okay with that. As long as you treat her right.

JOHNNY. I will. I promise.

(He takes out a comb and combs his hair.)

JACK. Funny how things change, huh?

JOHNNY. I know. I been havin' this really strange feeling, lately.

*(He offers the comb to **JACK**.)*

JACK. Thanks.

(He takes the comb and combs his hair.)

What kind of feeling?

JOHNNY. Well, I wasn't sure at first, but I finally figured it out.

(SONG - "Hoe Down")

(sings)

I'VE HAD LOTS OF FEELINGS
SOME GOOD AND SOME BAD
SOMETIMES I'VE BEEN HOPEFUL
AND OTHER TIMES SAD.

BUT LATELY I'VE BECOME AWARE
OF A BRAND NEW SENSATION
AND SUDDENLY I WAS STRUCK
WITH AN AMAZING, INCREDIBLE, ABSOLUTELY
   STUPENDOUS
REALIZATION —

I'M HAPPY.
I'M REALLY HAPPY.
I'M HAPPY AND IT MAKES ME FEEL JUST GRAND
OH YES, I'M HAPPY!
IT MIGHT SOUND SAPPY,
BUT HAPPINESS IS SOMETHING
I NEVER USED TO UNDERSTAND.

JACK. No kidding. Is that what that is?

JOHNNY. You feel it, too?

JACK. You mean when you want laugh and joke around and be nice to people you usually hate?

JOHNNY. That's it.

(sings)

YOU'RE HAPPY.

JACK.
YOU'RE RIGHT! I'M HAPPY
I FEEL LIKE EVERYTHING IS ABSOLUTELY GREAT.
I'M BLISSFUL
MY HEART IS THIS FULL
HAPPINESS IS SOMETHING
YOU SHOULD NEVER UNDER-ESTIMATE

(While the two leave, ISABEL and ANGELA enter with a chair [as if they're in her room] combing each other's hair while getting ready for the dance.)

ANGELA.
I'M HAPPY.
I'M REALLY HAPPY.
I'M HAPPY AND IT MAKES ME FEEL JUST GRAND
OH YES, I'M HAPPY!
IT MIGHT SOUND SAPPY,
BUT HAPPINESS IS SOMETHING
I NEVER USED TO UNDERSTAND.

ISABEL.
I USED TO BE GLOOMY
AND FILLED WITH DESPAIR
NOW I SEE RAINBOWS AND DON'T HAVE A CARE

I'M ECSTATIC
IT SOUNDS DRAMATIC
I FEEL LIKE SINGING AND DANCING ALL THE TIME.

BOTH.
BECAUSE I'M HAPPY, OH, SO HAPPY
HAPPINESS IS SOMETHING
THAT MAKES MY LIFE SUBLIME

*(Two separate groups of girls come in all getting ready for the dance. **MARY** and **YUSI** is one group while **MARIA**, **CHARLOTTE**, and **LOUISA** is the second.)*

MARY & YUSI.

I USED TO BE HOPELESS
WITHOUT A CLUE
THERE WAS NOTHING I COULD DO

MARIA, CHARLOTTE, & LOUISA.

I USED TO BE GLOOMY AND FILLED WITH DESPAIR
NOW I SEE RAINBOWS AND DON'T HAVE A CARE.

ALL FIVE GIRLS.

I'M SERIOUS JUST DELIRIOUS
FEEL LIKE DANCING ALL THE TIME
I'M HAPPY OH SO HAPPY
HAPPINESS IS SOMETHING THAT MAKES MY LIFE SUBLIME

*(The entire cast – except for **RACHEL**, **JESSIE**, and **LAURA** - make their way to the dance from different points on stage.)*

WE'RE HAPPY WERE REALLY HAPPY
WE'RE HAPPY AND IT MAKES US SMILE
WE'RE HAPPY IT MIGHT SOUND SAPPY
BUT HAPPINESS IS SOMETHING
YES IT'S THE ONE THING
HAPPINESS IS SOMETHING THAT MAKES OUR LIVES WORTH WHILE!!!

(Everyone enters and stands milling around waiting for the barn dance to begin.)

KATHY. Jack! Ray! Hey guys!

JACK. *(gives her a hug)* Hey Kathy!

JOHNNY. You're looking quite lovely tonight, Kathy.

KATHY. *(blushing)* What are you saying?

JOHNNY. You heard me. For once, can't you just take a compliment?

KATHY. But… listen…I…uh…thanks.

(For once, she feels shy.)

MARIA. Hey, how do I look? This blouse is brand new!

JACK. Lookin' pretty good, Angela.

MARIA. Jack, you have excellent taste!

YUSI. I got my dancin' shoes on but I'm not sure about this barn dance.

MARY. Yeah, it sounds a little corny.

MOLLY. It's not corny at all. It's fun and it's a town tradition.

MATT. We always have a barn dance at this time of year.

(**RACHEL, ANNIE,** and **JESSIE** enter, with **LAURA** on her crutches.)

LAURA. I really don't like going to dances. It's no fun to sit and watch all the time.

JESSIE. Maybe this time will be different, Laura.

LAURA It's no use, Jessie. I can't do it.

JESSIE. (to **RACHEL**) I told you this was a bad idea, trying to teach her to walk. It'll never work.

RACHEL. Give it a chance. You never know.

RAY. Hey, there's Rachel! And Annie!

RACHEL. Annie, over here!

CARLOS. (running in) Did I miss anything?

RAY. Nope, you're right on time.

CARLOS. You're not going to believe this, Ray, but I was learning how to milk a cow.

ANNIE. Seriously?

CARLOS. Yeah. I figure if I'm sticking around, I might as well help out, you know?

ANNIE. I know exactly.

RAY. Good for you, Carlos! I guess a few hot meals are changing your mind about this place.

CARLOS. Kind of.

MATT. All right, everyone, are you ready for a real good time? Choose your partners!

CARLOS. Annie?

ANNIE. Sure!

RAY. Come on, Molly, you seem like you'd be a good teacher!

MOLLY. Definitely one of the best. I mean, I'll try!

JACK. If I got to do this, Rachel, you are doing it with me!

RACHEL. It'll be fun, I think.

ISABEL. Hi Jessie…

JESSIE. Hello Isabel…

ISABEL. Um..Would you like to be partners?

JESSIE. …Yes…I would.

MATT. Okay Everybody! Let's get ready to doe si doe!

JOHNNY. Doe si doe? Is that English?

MATT. It's a dance step, you'll see.

*(Everyone pairs up except for **LAURA**. **JESSIE** and **RACHEL** are partners.)*

All right, folks!

Find your place

Grand Square

(the kids square dance as he calls out the steps)

Allemande.

Doe si doe. Promenade her.

Four hands square.

Round the corner. Doe si doe.

JACK. You call this dancing?

KATHY. I call it sleeping on my feet!

MOLLY. You don't like it?

CARLOS. It's so slow!

RACHEL. Hey, Laura! Why don't you come and join us?

LAURA. No, thanks.

JESSIE. I told you.

ANNIE. Maybe the next dance will inspire her.

MARY. Where we come from, the music has lot more beat.

RAY. You can say that again. A New York City beat.

JESSIE. What's that?

ANGELA. Shall we show 'em, guys?

ORPHANS. Yeah!

JOHNNY. *(grabs KATHY's hand and twirls her around)* Want to give it a go?

KATHY. You bet I would!

(SONG - "New York City Beat")

JOHNNY & KATHY. *(sing)*
WHEN YOU WAKE UP IN THE MORNING IN NEW YORK CITY,
YOU WILL SEE A SIGHT THAT'S OH SO PRETTY.
CROWDS ON THE SIDEWALK,
TRAFFIC IN THE STREET,
A-MOVIN' AND A-GROOVIN' TO THE NEW YORK CITY BEAT.

MARY.
YOU CAN TAKE A BUS IN NEW YORK CITY.
BUT IF YOU REALLY WANT THE NITTY GRITTY.
GO DOWN TO THE SUBWAY
OR SIMPLY USE YOUR FEET,
A-MOVIN' AND A-GROOVIN' TO THE NEW YORK CITY BEAT.

ANGELA AND YUSI.
THERE ARE PEOPLE IN TAXIS,
PEOPLE DRIVING CARS,
RUSHING TO REACH BUILDINGS
THAT ALMOST TOUCH THE STARS.

HARLEM KIDS.
IN THE FREEZING COLD WINTER
THE SUMMERTIME HEAT
WE'RE MOVIN' AND A-GROOVIN' TO THE NEW YORK CITY BEAT.

(The orphans do a dance number. RACHEL joins them. Then they pull in MATT, MOLLY, and JESSIE.)

(As they dance, LAURA sways to the music, caught by the rhythm. Finally, LAURA jumps up and joins them.)

JESSIE. Rachel! Look at Laura!

RACHEL. All right, Laura! I knew you could do it. You just needed a reason. Go, Laura, go!

(**RACHEL**, **JESSIE** and **LAURA** *dance a solo piece.*)

RACHEL, JESSIE, LAURA.
WE GOT PLACES TO GO
PEOPLE TO MEET.
A-MOVIN' AND A-GROOVIN' TO THE NEW YORK CITY BEAT.

(dance break)

ALL.
WE'RE FEELING REAL GOOD.
LIFE IS COMPLETE.
MOVIN' AND A-GROOVIN'
JUMPIN AND A PUMPIN
HOP HOP HOP AND A POP
TO THE NEW YORK CITY BEAT.

*(Everyone cheers each and hugs each other. Suddenly, **RACHEL** starts to feel dizzy.)*

RACHEL. Ohhh, my head!

MARY. Rachel, are you all right?

RACHEL. I don't know. The room is spinning. I feel so dizzy…I need to sit down…Ohhh…

(She faints and collapses to the floor.)

MARY. Rachel! Somebody help us!

(The kids rush over.)

KIDS. *(talk all at once)* What's the matter? What happened? Oh, my God! I don't know. She just fainted.

JACK. Stand back, give her some air. Let me take a look.

*(He examines **RACHEL** and gently slaps her cheek.)*

Rachel? Rachel, can you hear me?

JESSIE. *(terrified)* Is she dead?

JACK. Of course not! She's breathing just fine, but she won't wake up.

KATHY. Somebody call a doctor!

LAURA. There are no doctors in this town. They're all in the city.

MOLLY. There's no way to reach him at this hour.

JACK. Can't we bring her to him?

MATT. I suppose we could put her on the midnight train. But someone would have to go with her.

JESSIE. I will! I'll take Rachel to the doctor. I know where he lives because of going with Laura all the time.

JOHNNY. What time is it now?

MARY. Eleven thirty.

JOHNNY. Come on, everybody. Let's carry Rachel to the train.

(Lights fade as they all pick up **RACHEL** *and carry her off.)*

Scene 8 – Train Station

(RACHEL is carried and placed on a train seat. JESSIE sits down and faces the other kids.)

LAURA. Hurry back, Jessie. I'll miss you.

JESSIE. I'll miss you, too, Laura, and I am so proud of you.

KATHY. Yeah, and take good care of Rachel. Or you'll have me to answer to me when you get back!

JESSIE. I will.

ANGELA. When she wakes up, tell her how worried we were.

JESSIE. Okay.

ANNIE. Tell her we hope she feels better and to come back soon.

JESSIE. Sure.

CARLOS. And if there's anything either of you need, just let us know.

JESSIE. I will. And I'll also tell her what good friends you all are.

MOLLY. You've turned into a pretty good friend, yourself.

(They smile at each other.)

CONDUCTOR. All aboard! The Midnight train is leaving on Track Two in one minute.

JESSIE. Well, I guess this is it. Bye, everybody!

KIDS. *(waving)* Bye! So long! Good luck.

(The kids exit. JESSIE sits next to RACHEL, who is still unconscious.)

JESSIE. Don't worry, Rachel. Everything's going to be just fine. I'll make sure of it. *(yawns)* Gosh, I sure am tired. I think I'll just close my eyes for a few minutes.

(She closes her eyes and falls asleep.)

*(Lights fade as we hear a Musical Interlude of **MY LIFE** with sound of train moving.)*

Scene 9 – Rachel's Bedroom

(Lights up as the music ends. **RACHEL** *lies in bed next to* **JESSIE**. *She wakes up and looks around)*

RACHEL. Where am I? Oh, my God! I'm home. In my bedroom, in my own bed! *(sees* **JESSIE***)* Is that Jessie? What's she doing here? Jessie! Jessie, wake up.

JESSICA. *(sits up)* What's going on?

RACHEL. Jessie, don't get upset. But there's something I have to tell you. We're in the year 2004.

JESSICA. Of course we are. Why would I get upset about that?

RACHEL. But Jessie, we've traveled through time. You've left Laura behind.

JESSICA. Who's Laura? And why do you keep calling me, Jessie? You know I hate that name.

RACHEL. What should I call you?

JESSICA. Duh. How about Jessica?

RACHEL. You're *Jessica*?

JESSICA. That's not funny, Rachel. I know you're unhappy and you hate your life, but…

RACHEL. No, I'm not! I'm very happy and I really like myself! I'm a much better person than I thought.

JESSICA. Then you're not going to run away?

RACHEL. Run away?

JESSICA. Rachel, you asked me to sleep over last night because today you're planning to run away and start over, remember?

RACHEL. But I did run away. I was on the Orphan Train and then we were in Kansas and I helped Laura to walk and I discovered that I was just as good as anybody else.

JESSICA. What are you talking about?

RACHEL. Did I ever tell you what a good friend you are? And how much I appreciate you?

JESSICA. Now I definitely know that you're sick.

RACHEL. I feel great! I've never felt better. Come on, let's get dressed and go out.

JESSICA. Where?

RACHEL. Who knows? Anywhere. Life is a beautiful adventure and there are all kinds of new people to meet. Let's go!

(SONG - "Things Aren't Always What They Seem [Reprise]")

(sings)

SEE A TREE IN WINTER,
ITS BRANCHES ARE BARE.
IT'S EASY TO SUSPECT
THAT NOTHING'S GROWING THERE.

JESSICA.

BUT WAIT UNTIL SPRING
AND LIKE OUT OF A DREAM.

RACHEL & JESSICA.

THERE'S A TREE FULL OF BLOSSOMS.
THING'S AREN'T ALWAYS WHAT THEY SEEM.

(They exit with their arms around each other.)

(Cast enters for Finale and sings the end of "Tree in Winter" starting with "Don't Make Assumptions...")

(curtain)

www.ingramcontent.com/pod-product-compliance
Lightning Source LLC
Chambersburg PA
CBHW071415290426
44108CB00014B/1837